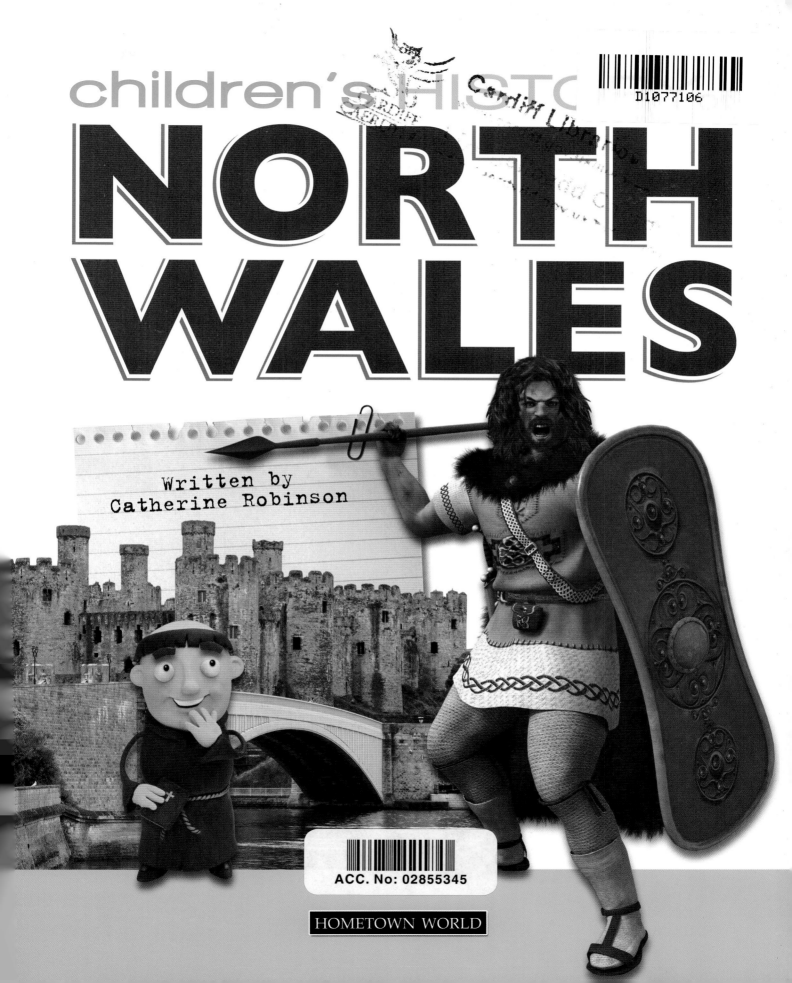

children's HISTORY

NORTH WALES

Written by
Catherine Robinson

HOMETOWN WORLD

How well do you know your town?

Have you ever wondered what it would have been like living in North Wales when the Romans arrived? What about partying in the Great Chamber of Plas Mawr during Tudor times? This book tells the story of your town, with all the important and exciting things that have taken place there.

Want to hear the other good bits? You will love this book! Some rather brainy folk have worked on it to make sure it's fun and informative. So what are you waiting for? Peel back the pages and be amazed at what happened in North Wales.

Timeline shows which period (dates and people) each spread is talking about

Clear informative text

Hometown facts to amaze you!

'Spot this!' game with hints on something to find in North Wales

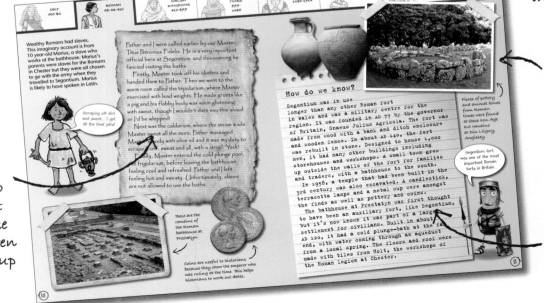

Go back in time to read what it was like for children growing up in North Wales.

Intriguing photos

Each period in the book ends with a summary explaining how we know about the past.

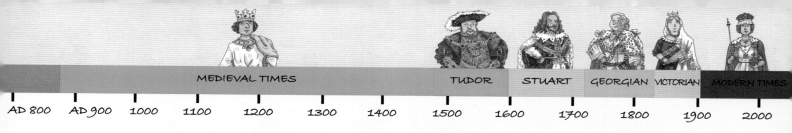

Contents

The Hill Fort

It is a sunny September afternoon on Moel Hiraddug. Ffion is sitting outside her roundhouse, making dye from woad leaves in a large iron pot. The smoke from the fire makes her eyes sting, and she rubs them with hands stained bright blue from the woad. She will use the dye on a woollen cloak she has woven for her husband, the chieftain. The smell of rabbit stew wakens her baby son, Huw, who is lying beside her on a wolf hide. It's dinnertime!

Iron Age Celts

The Iron Age Celts lived across Europe from about 600 BC. The name Iron Age comes from the discovery of a new metal called iron. The clues dug up by archaeologists show how good the Iron Age Celts were at making metal objects, including weapons, pots and jewellery.

Their settlements were built on hills to keep invaders out. They had high walls and deep ditches, and contained roundhouses built of wattle and daub, with straw roofs. There are many remains of Iron Age hill forts in North Wales. Moel Hiraddug is near Dyserth, in Denbighshire. Nearby is Penycloddiau, one of the largest hill forts in Wales. Sometimes the settlements were built on top of even earlier sites, such as at Gop Hill near Prestatyn.

You wouldn't find me collecting dung for the roundhouse walls. I'm a warrior!

Guess what smelly ingredient was used to make the walls of a roundhouse...

Roundhouse walls were made from woven branches covered in mud mixed with straw, horsehair and... animal poo!

Celtic Life

Roman writers tell us that the Celts lived in tribes. They wore gold jewellery, loved to drink wine and were fierce fighters – even the women! They used plants and berries to dye their clothes bright colours with stripes and checks. They used blue woad not just for their clothes, but to paint patterns all over their bodies too. Iron Age Celts were also farmers, growing corn and keeping animals such as sheep, goats, cows and pigs.

Celts worshipped their gods through sacrifice, giving them valuable food, animals or even people, to keep them happy. They also sacrificed weapons to the gods by throwing them into lakes, rivers and bogs – places they considered special. Celtic priests were called druids. The druids were particularly powerful on Anglesey and rallied local people to fight against the Romans when they invaded the island.

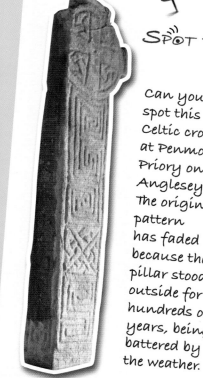

SPOT THIS!

Can you spot this Celtic cross at Penmon Priory on Anglesey? The original pattern has faded because the pillar stood outside for hundreds of years, being battered by the weather.

This brooch was found during excavations at Moel Hiraddug in the early 1960s.

Celtic soldiers had white spiky hair because they put lime on it, just as we use hair gel today!

We're very good at making jewellery and colourful checked clothes.

Arts and Crafts

The Celts were skilled craftworkers as well as fearsome warriors. The most important soldiers wore fancy bronze helmets and had shields decorated with signs and patterns. They wore special necklaces, called torcs, made of iron or precious metal. Women wore beautifully made brooches, bracelets and necklaces too.

Celtic patterns can also be found on stone crosses and monuments both old and new, for example on Llanddwyn Island, Anglesey and at St Tudno's church on Llandudno's Great Orme. Celtic crafts, stories and music have influenced artists and craftsmen for centuries.

CELT
500 BC

ROMAN
AD 43-410

WELSH
KINGDOMS
410-877

MEDIEVAL
TIMES
877-
1485

This is what 10 year-old Gwyr, a blacksmith's son, might have said about a day at the hill fort. He probably would have spoken Brythonic – a Celtic language spoken in Wales and southern Britain.

Invaders beware! I'm the best slingshot in all of Cymru!

Today, traders came to the settlement wanting pots and shields and bringing animal skins and grain to trade for them. I was practising slingshot with Medyr and Osian. At first, I thought the strangers struggling up the hill were invaders, but they carried no weapons. Then they asked to see Father's finest work, and were very pleased by the quality. I felt very proud to be Gwyr ap Gwilym – the son of Gwilym, the blacksmith.

Soon after that my sister, Gwawr, poked her head in and asked if I was coming to the spring with her and her friends. They were going to make an offering, she said, to give thanks for the birth of the chieftain's new son.

"I'm busy," I told her scornfully. I wanted to add that I am a blacksmith's son and that celebrating babies is for women, but I managed to hold my tongue. I thought Father might chase me around his workshop with hot tongs for being disrespectful to my sister!

These blacksmith's tongs are part of the Llyn Cerrig Bach hoard found on Anglesey.

Aerial photographs are very useful to historians and archaeologists. This one shows the Celtic hill fort at Penycloddiau.

The account on the right is from the Roman emperor Julius Caesar, who wrote about the Iron Age Celts and how they fought in battle.

Me? Afraid of those terrifying blue men, the Celts? Never!

All of them dye themselves with woad, which occasions a bluish colour, and thereby have a more terrible appearance in fight... This is how they fight with their chariots: Firstly, they drive about in all directions and throw their weapons and generally break the ranks of the enemy with the very dread of their horses and the noise of their wheels; and when they have worked themselves in between the troops of horse, they leap from their chariots and engage on foot.

How do we know?

The early Celts did not read or write so left behind no books about themselves, but luckily the Romans did. We base some of what we know about Iron Age Celts on Roman writings such as the quote from Julius Caesar, above. A Roman historian called Tacitus also wrote about the Celts.

The remains of many hill forts tell us more about life in the Iron Age. For example, Gop Hill has the largest burial mound in Wales. Skeletons from 4300 to 2300 BC, known as the Neolithic Age, were found in caves there. Moel Hiraddug was excavated several times between 1954 and 1980, when archaeologists discovered more about the hill fort's buildings and defences, as well as a store of sling stones.

At Llyn Cerrig Bach on Anglesey, workers clearing ground to build the RAF base at Valley in 1942 found more than 150 bronze and iron objects, including spears, shields and swords. It's now thought these were put in the lake by the druids as offerings to their gods.

The Celts ruled over North Wales for hundreds of years, long before the Romans turned up.

CELT
500 BC

ROMAN
AD 43-410

WELSH
KINGDOMS
410-877

MEDIEVAL
TIMES
877–
1485

At Segontium

Cassius is cold, tired and hungry. He has been based at Segontium fort for several months now. He came from a country far away in the south with the rest of his regiment. Their main task is to repair the fort's aqueduct, which channels water from the well to the whole fort. He has spent the day replacing a broken pipe with a new whole one. Autumn in this country is cold and it never seems to stop drizzling. Cassius is looking forward to having supper indoors in the warm. Perhaps he will visit the bathhouse later, and relax with his comrades.

The Romans Arrive

The Romans first settled in Britain in AD 43. Their emperor, Claudius, wanted to show his power by taking over foreign countries. Roman forces reached Wales in AD 48. Six years later they attacked Anglesey, which they wanted to control because it was excellent farming land, and contained many important minerals such as copper and lead. Segontium fort was built around AD 77 near what is now Caernarfon, overlooking the Menai Straits. It protected Anglesey against Irish raiders and pirates.

There are many signs of Roman occupation in the area, including remains of a tile and pottery factory in Holt, Denbighshire; a lead and silver mine at Pentre, Flintshire; a military station at Caerhun, Gwynedd; and a Roman bathhouse at Prestatyn.

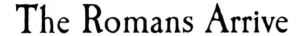

Historians think the Roman fort at Segontium would have looked like this.

The Roman Army

The Roman army consisted of groups of soldiers called legions. There were around 5,000 soldiers in a legion, each with its own name, number, fortress and emblem. There were around 30 legions in Europe and the 20th Legion was based just over the border in Chester, then known as Deva. Legions were made up of smaller groups. A century consisted of around 80 men and was commanded by a centurion. Six centuries made a cohort, and ten cohorts made up a legion. As well as soldiers, a legion had engineers, doctors and other workers.

Segontium was built for auxiliary solders. They were not local men but came from tribes across Europe, signing up for at least 25 years in return for Roman citizenship.

SPOT THIS!

This is a Roman well at the Segontium fort. Can you spot the real thing?

Roman soldiers were not allowed to marry until AD 197, when the law changed.

This gold brooch was found at Segontium.

Auxiliary soldiers and nurses are named after our Latin word for 'help'... auxilia.

Roman Numerals

I	= 1	VIII	= 8
II	= 2	IX	= 9
III	= 3	X	= 10
IV	= 4	L	= 50
V	= 5	C	= 100
VI	= 6	D	= 500
VII	= 7	M	= 1,000

After the Romans

Segontium was occupied until AD 394. The Roman soldiers finally left Britain around AD 410, but we can still see Roman influence today on lots of things we do or have. For example, British laws and government are based on Roman models, and the Romans invented the modern calendar. Their language, Latin, influenced many European languages, including English. The Romans also invented central heating, aqueducts, concrete, road drainage, public parks and libraries.

Can you think of examples of when Roman numerals are used today?

CELT
500 BC

ROMAN
AD 43-410

WELSH
KINGDOMS
410-877

MEDIEVAL
TIMES
877-
1485

Wealthy Romans had slaves. This imaginary account is from 9 year-old Marius, a slave who works at the bathhouse. Marius's parents were slaves for the Romans in Chester but they were all chosen to go with the army when they travelled to Segontium. Marius is likely to have spoken in Latin.

Scraping off dirt and sweat... I get all the best jobs!

Father and I were called earlier by our Master, Titus Petronius Fidelis. He is a very important official here at Segontium, and this evening he fancied visiting the baths.

Firstly, Master took off his clothes and handed them to Father. Then we went to the warm room called the tepidarium, where Master exercised with lead weights. He made grunts like a pig and his flabby body was soon glistening with sweat, though I wouldn't dare say this aloud or I'd be whipped!

Next was the caldarium, where the steam made Master sweat all the more. Father massaged Master's body with olive oil and it was my duty to scrape it off, sweat and all, with a strigil. Yuck!

Finally, Master entered the cold plunge pool, the frigidarium, before leaving the bathhouse feeling cool and refreshed. Father and I left feeling hot and sweaty. Unfortunately, slaves are not allowed to use the baths.

These are the remains of the Roman bathhouse at Prestatyn.

Coins are useful to historians because they show the emperor who was ruling at the time. This helps historians to work out dates.

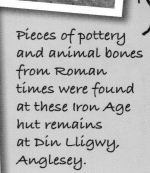

How do we know?

Segontium was in use longer than any other Roman fort in Wales and was a military centre for the region. It was founded in AD 77 by the governor of Britain, Gnaeus Julius Agricola. The fort was made from wood with a bank and ditch enclosure and wooden fence. In about AD 140, the fort was rebuilt in stone. Designed to house 1,000 men, it had many other buildings including storehouses and workshops. A small town grew up outside the walls of the fort for families and traders, with a bathhouse to the south.

In 1958, a temple that had been built in the 3rd century was also excavated. A candlestick, terracotta lamps and a metal cup were amongst the finds as well as pottery and coins.

The bathhouse at Prestatyn was first thought to have been an auxiliary fort, like Segontium, but it's now known it was part of a larger settlement for civilians. Built in about AD 120, it had a cold plunge-bath at the far end, with water coming through an aqueduct from a local spring. The floors and roof were made with tiles from Holt, the workshops of the Roman legion at Chester.

Pieces of pottery and animal bones from Roman times were found at these Iron Age hut remains at Din Lligwy, Anglesey.

Segontium fort was one of the most important Roman forts in Britain.

CELT
500 BC

ROMAN
AD 43-410

WELSH
KINGDOMS
410-877

MEDIEVAL
TIMES
877-
1485

Mighty Maelgwn

News of an uprising has reached Maelgwn Hir at his court in Deganwy. He will lose no time in setting about the scoundrels and rogues who dare to question his rule. They'll be sorry! Afterwards, perhaps he'll pay one of his favourite bards to write a poem, set to the music of a harp and praising the king... All hail Maelgwn, mighty King of Gwynedd!

A Celtic Country

After the last Roman soldiers left, Britain had many kings, each ruling over a tribe and fighting for the land of other tribes. A mixture of people from north Germany, Denmark and northern Holland invaded eastern Britain. Historians call them Anglo-Saxons. Some came to Britain to fight, but others came peacefully, to find land to farm.

Meanwhile, the Celts stayed in the west, resisting other tribes and the invading Anglo-Saxons, who never conquered Wales. This is clearly seen today in the Welsh language, unlike English which was influenced by the Roman, Anglo-Saxon and later Norman invaders. Many places in Wales have names containing Celtic words. Common examples are *pen* (head), *llan* (church), *tref* (town), *porth* (port) and *bod* (dwelling).

Deganwy Castle

In the 6th century, a warrior called Maelgwn built his castle above what is now Deganwy, near Llandudno. It survived for over a thousand years. Overlooking Anglesey, Snowdonia and the Conwy Valley, it allowed Maelgwn to control Gwynedd. He was one of the best-known Welsh rulers of the age, and supported the Welsh poets and songwriters, called bards.

Where's the battle, Maelgwn? I'll fight with you!

Maelgwn's castle once stood here.

Offa's Dyke

Offa was a powerful English ruler in the 8th century. He had a huge earth structure built along the entire Welsh border, called Offa's Dyke. It had a bank and a 4 metre-wide ditch facing Wales. Some believe Offa built it to keep Eliseg, King of Powys, out of England. Offa's Dyke made people feel more Welsh. It separated them from England and, soon afterwards, most of Wales was under the power of its own ruler.

As well as his dyke, King Offa left another inheritance. He issued the first silver penny coins to bear the British king's head, known as 'Offa's pennies'.

SPOT THIS!
Eliseg's Pillar in Valle Crucis, near Llangollen, has a message urging the people of Powys to fight the Anglo-Saxons by fire and sword.

Offa's Dyke is Britain's longest ancient monument. Bits of it are missing but you can walk along the whole 185 km-long path.

Rhodri Mawr

In the late 9th century, another set of invaders came to settle in Britain, this time from Scandinavia. These invaders are known as the Vikings. In North Wales, one of the most famous kings was Rhodri Mawr (the Great). He was called this because he defeated the Vikings in AD 856. Rhodri Mawr added to his lands of Gwynedd and, by the time he died in AD 877, most of Wales was ruled by him.

How do we know?

A historian called Gildas wrote about Maelgwn in the 6th century, although he didn't think much of him — he described Maelgwn as a drunken bully who murdered his own uncle so he could be king himself!

Welsh poetry dates from the 6th century, earlier than any other form of literature in northern Europe. Although the language is an early form of Welsh and is hard to understand, the poems tell us about events, people and legends in Welsh history. Taliesin, the foster son of Maelgwn's nephew, wrote a collection of poetry in the 6th century that is well-known today.

Excavations at Deganwy Castle in the 1960s show it was occupied in the 5th and 6th centuries and, in 1979, a hoard of 204 silver pennies was found nearby.

CELT
500 BC

ROMAN
AD 43-410

WELSH
KINGDOMS
410-877

MEDIEVAL
TIMES
877-
1485

Slate for Conwy

Bryn clicks his teeth and hurries his horses along. His wagon, laden with Llanberis slate, is bound for the English king's new castle at Conwy; his master had stressed the importance of getting it to the town and out again by sundown, or risk imprisonment. Welshmen are forbidden in the town by night, he'd said. Bryn is a worried man...

Map of Medieval Wales

Gwynedd

N

Powys

OFFA'S DYKE

Deheubarth

Brycheiniog

Gwent

Morgannwg

0 25 50
Kilometres

In medieval times, Wales was divided into several kingdoms, including Gwynedd and Powys in the north.

Llywelyn Fawr

In 1066, the Normans took control of England under their king, William the Conqueror. They arrived in Wales around 1070. By 1100, the Welsh people had risen in revolt and driven the Normans out of Gwynedd. Some areas were still under the control of Norman lords, in their castles. These lords became known as the Marcher Lords and they continued to fight for power in Wales.

Owain Gwynedd was an important ruler in the 12th century. His grandson, Llywelyn, later became master of Gwynedd. In 1205, Llywelyn married Siwan (Joan), daughter of King John of England. He seized more land and became even more powerful. Eventually he would be known as Llywelyn Fawr (the Great).

Llywelyn Ein Llyw Olaf

Llywelyn ap Gruffudd was the grandson of Llywelyn Fawr. He gave himself the name 'Prince of Wales' and, in 1267, King Henry III recognized this title. Llywelyn took control of several less powerful rulers in Wales. Llywelyn was in charge of about three quarters of the land in the country, including most of North Wales. He has since become known as Llywelyn Ein Llyw Olaf (the Last).

Edward's Castles

In 1282, King Edward I of England decided he wanted complete control of Wales. He attacked Wales, and Llywelyn Ein Llyw Olaf was killed. This was the end of Wales being independent from England.

Next, Edward weakened Welsh laws and brought in English ones instead. In 1284, his Statute of Rhuddlan divided the mighty Gwynedd into several smaller counties, with sheriffs in charge.

Edward also repaired and rebuilt castles across Wales. In the north, he built major ones at Conwy, Caernarfon, Harlech and Beaumaris, forming an 'Iron Ring' to prevent Welsh attack. Towns grew up around the castles, as they had around Roman forts.

King Edward I was not popular in Wales. He showed no respect for Welsh tradition and heritage and built over the burial place of Llewelyn Fawr at the old monastery in Aberconwy. In 1301, Edward awarded his son the title 'Prince of Wales'. Since then, the heir to the throne of England has traditionally been given that title.

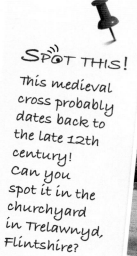

SPOT THIS! This medieval cross probably dates back to the late 12th century! Can you spot it in the churchyard in Trelawnyd, Flintshire?

Edward I brought in English laws and sheriffs. He's not a popular man.

Bangor takes its name from the fence that enclosed the monastery, called a bangor.

Cistercian monks once lived here, at Valle Crucis Abbey near Llangollen.

Medieval Monks

The Norman-English thought the early Welsh church was too independent and different from their own Christian faith, so they encouraged monks called Benedictines to settle in Wales. But the Welsh turned the tables by starting monasteries for Cistercian monks instead. Cistercians liked their monasteries in quiet places and preferred the simple life. The Cistercians supported the Welsh rulers who gave them land, which they needed for farming and raising sheep. As with the castles, towns grew up around these monasteries, and trade began to grow as money spread.

CELT
500 BC

ROMAN
AD 43-410

WELSH
KINGDOMS
410-877

MEDIEVAL
TIMES
877-
1485

The constable of a medieval castle looked after it when the owner was away. Records tell us that in 1394 the constable at Conwy was nobleman John de Holland, who lived with his family in the towers overlooking the drawbridge.

Here is an imaginary diary entry by his eldest daughter, Constance.

> I thought younger brothers and sisters were meant to be fun.

The King is to visit, and I was told to mind the little ones while Mother was busy getting things ready for the occasion. I doubt the King will set one royal foot inside our towers, but Mother was having the floor rushes changed, the candlewicks trimmed and so on.

Richard took himself off to the stables to pet the horses and Alice was quite happy playing with her doll, but John cried so much I feared he'd hurt himself. I carried him down to the kitchen garden to show him the flowers, but still he cried.

Finally, Mary the maid came out with a piece of gingerbread for John. She took him from me to comfort him and said that he needed fresh swaddling cloths. So I took him back to Mother.

When I am grown, I will have a rich husband and no children.

The cost to Edward I of building Conwy Castle was around £15,000 – that's over £6 million today!

In medieval times, babies were wrapped like this to keep them still. People also believed it helped their backs to grow straight.

Conwy Castle is one of the key castles built by King Edward I to control the Welsh.

Plan of Conwy Castle

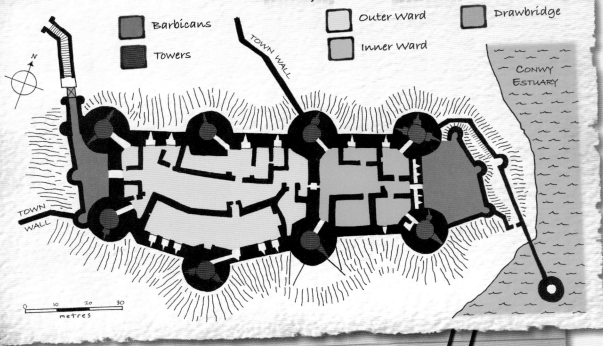

Barbicans

Towers

Outer Ward

Inner Ward

Drawbridge

TOWN WALL

CONWY ESTUARY

TOWN WALL

N

0   10   20   30
metres

Conwy is an example of a concentric castle. It has rings of walls, one inside the other, with towers along them.

How do we know?

Edward I built strong defensive walls because he not only brought in English builders, but also a whole population of English settlers! They were protected by the walls from the local Welsh population who were often forbidden inside the towns. Life outside the castle walls was hard for the local people, who were forced to be obedient to the English.

Edward's Welsh castles were built from local materials – including slate from the ancient quarries near Llanberis – and designed by the master mason James of St George, from Savoy, in modern Italy. In a letter to the king's Exchequer, when building Beaumaris Castle, he said: 'In case you wonder where so much money could go in a week, we've needed – 400 masons, together with 2,000 less skilled workmen, 100 carts, 60 wagons and 30 boats bringing stone and sea coal; 200 quarrymen; 30 smiths; and carpenters for the joists and floorboards...'

English kings were trying to gain more power in Wales during medieval times.

Party Time!

It's hot inside the Great Hall at Plas Mawr. The remains of a lavish feast have been cleared away and the merry guests have taken to the dancefloor. Their wealthy host, Robert Wynn, has been eager to show his guests a good time. He was very pleased with their reaction when they first entered his new house and saw its grand plasterwork and decorations. One of them said it was the finest house in all of Wales!

Owain Glyndwr

In the early 15th century, an important rebellion took place against the new English king, Henry IV. The rebellion was led by Owain Glyndwr. By 1405, almost all of Wales recognized Owain's power. Owain wrote a letter to the king of France, asking for support and listing his aims for Wales. He wanted two Welsh universities; priests to speak fluent Welsh; and all money raised by Welsh churches to stay in Wales. He also wanted Henry IV to be excluded from the Welsh church. Although it took the country a long time to recover from Owain Glyndwr's revolt, he is now recognized as a national hero because he encouraged a sense of being Welsh.

It was Glyndwr's dreams for Wales that earned Henry Tudor support. Henry Tudor was the grandson of Owain Tudur, a Welsh soldier and nobleman who

The Tudor Rose is a symbol of the Tudor family.

The Tudors ruled over England and Wales for 118 years.

married Henry V's widow. Owain's father, Tudur ap Geronwy, came from Anglesey. Calling himself 'Y Mab Darogan' or 'Son of Destiny', Henry promised to make Owain Glyndwr's dreams a reality. With Welsh help, he defeated Richard III at the Battle of Bosworth in 1485 and became King Henry VII.

The Act of Union

Henry VII's son became King Henry VIII and passed the Act of Union in 1536. This meant that Wales effectively became part of England, with English law in the courts and English as the official language. The Tudors brought peace after many years of wars and during their reign encouraged new religious ideas and exploration overseas.

SPOT THIS!

This Tudor Rose is in the middle of some fancy plasterwork – can you spot it at Plas Mawr, in Conwy?

Henry VIII wanted Wales and England to unite.

In 1568, a large Eisteddfod was held at Caerwys in Flintshire, on the orders of Queen Elizabeth I.

Plas Mawr is still decorated like it was in Tudor times.

A New World

Medieval towns such as Bangor, Caernarfon and Conwy grew during Tudor times. Bangor Grammar School, now known as Friars School, was established in 1557. People were moving from the countryside into towns like this. More travel led to more trading, with merchants and craftworkers becoming richer.

In the late 1500s, one wealthy merchant called Robert Wynn built a mansion in Conwy. Wynn liked extravagant things, travelled a lot and enjoyed having big parties. His mansion was called Plas Mawr and, today, it is one of the best examples of an Elizabethan house in Britain.

Most people in Tudor times were not rich like Robert Wynn. Life for the poor was full of problems. Towns were becoming overcrowded, causing danger from fire and allowing diseases to spread easily. Roads were uneven, muddy tracks and travelling was difficult.

Here's what one of Robert Wynn's children, Agnes, might have said about a big party at Plas Mawr in Tudor times. Agnes is likely to have been brought up to speak English because she was from a rich family.

Banging this drum against my tummy is not a good idea after all that food!

Yesterday, Mother and Father had twenty guests for dinner. Cook prepared a wonderful banquet of six courses, with all manner of meats, stuffed chickens, fish, venison pies, sweetmeats, and plums stewed in rosewater. In the centre of the table was a peacock made of marchpane, with real peacock feathers!

Afterwards there was dancing in the Great Hall to a consort of recorders and viols. They danced pavans, galliards and almains; one of the musicians told me the music was written by the great composer Master John Dowland. How wonderful it sounded, how pretty the dancing, how colourful the ladies' gowns! I would love to play the viol at a Plas Mawr party. But I fear I only have skill enough to bang a drum, and that badly…

Whole Baked Carpe with Spices and Prunes

Take off the Scales and take forth the Gall and with Cloves, mace and salte, season it and take corans and prunes and put about the carpe and take butter and put it upon him and let him bake two hours.

This is a real Tudor recipe. A carp is a type of fish and corans are currants.

Lots of new foods and spices were brought back from overseas during Tudor times.

Marchpane is what the Tudors called marzipan.

Can you imagine staying in a real Tudor castle? Gwydir Castle is now a home and guesthouse.

Gwydir Castle belongs to the Wynn family, descendants of ancient kings of Gwynedd.

North Wales was a peaceful place to live in Tudor and Stuart times.

How do we know?

The village of Penmynydd, where Owain Tudur was born, still has Tudor connections. St Gredifael's Church is the burial place of Gronw Fychan, one of Tudur ap Geronwy's sons. The church once had beautiful windows with original Tudor stained glass, but they were destroyed in 2007.

Gwydir Castle, near Llanrwst, is an important Tudor house. It was rebuilt around 1490 by Mareddud of Gwydir, a leading supporter of Henry VII, and the first member of the Wynn family in North Wales. In the 1570s it was the home of Morris Wynn and his wife, Catrin Berain, a cousin of Elizabeth I. Catrin had so many children and grandchildren that she became known as Mam Cymru (Mother of Wales).

Plas Mawr is full of extravagant detail such as plasterwork ceilings, friezes and carvings. Robert Wynn's initials are found everywhere, to remind visitors who was the master of the mansion, and how amazingly rich he was.

At the Quarry

It's 6 am and Gwilym has just started work. Twelve hours in the dressing shed lie ahead of him, splitting the heavy mass into neat roofing slates. By the end of his shift he'll be filthy from the dust, and he knows his cough will be troubling him. But Elen will have hot water waiting at home, and hot broth to ease the coughing. He's lucky – at least he's not out in the drizzle on the slippery quarry face, using explosives to blast the slate from the earth...

Victorian boys wore the same as girls until they were six or seven years old!

Industrial Revolution

During the late 18th century, science and technology advanced very quickly. The use of steam-powered machines in mills and factories led to small villages suddenly becoming large towns, and then cities.

Slate quarried from Dinorwic, near Llanberis, had been used at the Segontium fort and at Conwy Castle. But there was now a huge demand for slates to roof the houses built for industrial workers, and also the factories themselves.

By the 1870s, Dinorwic quarry employed over 3,000 men. Wales produced over 80 per cent of all British slates in this period and North Wales was the biggest producer. The Welsh slate trade reached its peak in 1898, with 17,000 men producing 485,000 tonnes of slate!

This old postcard shows workers at Dinorwic quarry in the late 1800s.

...1768 COPPER FOUND AT MYNYDD PARYS...1837 QUEEN VICTORIA IS CROWNED...

Copper and Railways

In 1768, vast amounts of copper were found at Mynydd Parys on Anglesey, and mining began. By 1793, Amlwch's port had become so busy that parliament voted to enlarge it. In 1801, Amlwch was the fifth largest town in Wales and the world's leading copper mine.

In 1826, Conwy Suspension Bridge was built by a famous engineer called Thomas Telford. It was one of the first road suspension bridges in the world. Telford also built a new post road from London to Wales. Holyhead became an important port for the Royal Mail, with post being dispatched from Holyhead to and from Dublin.

Railways – originally built to transport goods – spread rapidly and seaside holidays became popular. Llandudno was built in 1846 as a holiday resort. Its Victorian attractions such as the pier, donkey rides on the beach and Punch and Judy shows can still be enjoyed today.

These children are watching the Codman family's Punch and Judy show in Llandudno in about 1900.

PROFESSOR CODMANs WOODEN HEADED FOLLIES *Punch & Judy*

Spot this!

A pair of crossed foxes was the symbol of the Williams family at Bodelwyddan. Can you spot this picture on floor tiles at the castle?

Rich and Poor

Queen Victoria was on the throne for 64 years. During her reign their were huge changes in British society, but rich and poor Victorians led very different lives. The wealthy led lives of luxury, in big houses, such as Bodelwyddan Castle near Rhyl, with heating, lighting and servants.

Poor Victorians had a much harder time, working long hours, with unhealthy living conditions, little food and much illness and disease. Poor children didn't go to school. Instead they had to work a 12-hour day, just like adults, sometimes from the age of seven and often in terrible conditions.

I wanted to make Britain the richest, most powerful country in the world.

CELT 500 BC

ROMAN AD 43-410

WELSH KINGDOMS
410-877

MEDIEVAL TIMES
877-1485

The Chester–Holyhead railway line opened in 1848. The branch line to Llandudno followed 10 years later, when Bodelwyddan Castle was home to Sir John Hay Williams and his family. This is what Grace, aged 11, might have written in her diary about a weekend visit to Bodelwyddan with her mother and elder sister, Lily.

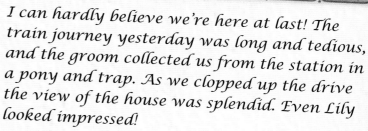

I bet I could fill a whole diary in the time it takes Lily to get into her corset.

I can hardly believe we're here at last! The train journey yesterday was long and tedious, and the groom collected us from the station in a pony and trap. As we clopped up the drive the view of the house was splendid. Even Lily looked impressed!

Once inside, Mama introduced us to her relatives, Sir John and Lady Sarah. Then Miss Thomas, the nanny, took me upstairs to meet Margaret and Maud, who are almost the same age as me. We've already become good friends.

Lily has her own room because, as she regularly reminds me, she is a young lady of nearly 18. She also has a lady's maid to attend to her every need. While Margaret, Maud and I played card games in the nursery, followed by high tea and bed, Lily had gallons of water carried upstairs for her bath, followed by a formal dinner with elegant adult company. She wore her new pale pink evening gown, made especially for the occasion.

Sometimes I wish I was Lily, nearly 18 and having Mama find a handsome husband for me. But then I remember the corset Lily has to struggle into each morning, and am glad I am still me!

Sir John Hay Williams spent a lot of money on Bodelwyddan to make it look more like a castle.

TUDOR AND STUART
1485-1714

GEORGIAN 1714-1837

VICTORIAN 1837-1901

MODERN TIMES
1902-NOW

You can walk inside these cottages at the National Slate Museum to see how quarryworkers lived.

This statue in Penmaenmawr shows Prime Minister William Gladstone, who holidayed there for over 40 years.

How do we know?

In 1830, Sir John Hay Williams inherited Bodelwyddan. Sir John kept detailed diaries of his activities. He also collected unusual plants and introduced heated outdoor walls to protect delicate fruit trees, almost fifty years before the house had heating! The 1851 census showed there were 23 staff at Bodelwyddan to look after just four members of the family.

By contrast, life for the slate quarrymen was hard, and often short. Life expectancy was just 52 years because accidents and injury were common, and slate dust caused lung disease. Dinorwic and Penrhyn quarries were the largest in Wales, possibly in the world. The owner of Penrhyn was so rich from selling slate, and also sugar from Jamaica, that he had Penrhyn Castle built near Bangor. Yet the quarrymen's work was difficult, dangerous and poorly paid. They often worked underground by the light of a single candle, or dangling from ropes high above the rock face.

We can learn a lot about Victorian life in North Wales from reading Welsh-language novels that were written at the time.

Life in North Wales was very different for the rich and the poor.

CELT
500 BC

ROMAN
AD 43-410

WELSH
KINGDOMS
410-877

MEDIEVAL
TIMES
877-
1485

Evacuated!

Brian wraps his arm around his little sister, Elsie. Both children are still carrying their suitcases and gas masks. They have just arrived from the community hall, where they waited with all the other evacuees from Liverpool to be taken to their new home. They are introduced to Owena, who lives here. Owena thinks it must be very hard to be sent away from home, not knowing when you would see your Mum and Dad again.

An American plane called 'Bachelor's Baby' crashed into the mountains near Penmaenmawr.

SP🔊T THIS!

'Bachelor's Baby' crashed in North Wales in 1944, killing five US airmen and their dog, Booster. This memorial marks the spot where they died.

Wartime in North Wales

World War Two took place from 1939 to 1945. While other parts of Britain suffered German bombing raids, North Wales got off lightly because there were no obvious targets such as big ports or factories. Important places, such as the BBC at Bangor and the Ministry of Food at Colwyn Bay, escaped bombing. Tragedy still struck the area though, with occasional bombs falling in places such as Llandudno and Abergele. Several air crews from Britain, the USA and Germany crashed their planes into the mountains or sea while training, or in bad weather.

It was difficult to get certain foods during the war, and rationing hit hard. But because the area was relatively safe, many children were evacuated there from Merseyside, and even as far as London. One London art gallery sent precious paintings to be stored secretly at Penrhyn Castle. Some other art treasures from London were taken to quarries at Blaenau Ffestiniog in vehicles disguised as chocolate delivery vans!

There's so much open space here. I can't wait to explore!

William Hunt was 13 when he was sent from Liverpool to Penmaenmawr. The account below is from his own words.

Life for the evacuees was peaceful, and we were well taken care of by our hosts. We enjoyed the beauty…the hillsides and the mountains, the streams. The evacuee's life in North Wales was a most pleasant and healthy one. We went to the local mountain range and walked for miles along pathways. We went out sometimes all day to collect wild bilberries on the mountain slopes… It was truly an ideal life for energetic boys.

How do we know?

A lot of children were evacuated to North Wales from Liverpool, a big target for German bombing. In September 1939, at the start of the war, an entire school — the Liverpool Blue Coat school — was evacuated to Beaumaris, on Anglesey.

Some evacuees were unhappy. Their host families were unkind, using them as unpaid labour and not feeding them properly. But others enjoyed their new lives away from the city. Many evacuees wrote letters to their families back home. Others kept diaries or have passed on stories to younger generations.

Closing Quarries

In wartime Britain, most men between 18 and 51 years old were called up for military service. Only those who were unfit or did certain jobs were excused. The slate industry wasn't considered essential so thousands of quarrymen went off to fight.

The demand for Welsh slate dropped because it was cheaper to get it from other countries, or to use roof tiles instead. All of this meant the slate industry never recovered, and by the end of the war more than half the quarries were closed.

Many men never returned from the war. It was a very sad time.

Since the War

In 1956, a secondary school called Ysgol Glan Clwyd opened in Rhyl. It was the first secondary school where all lessons were taught in Welsh.

A year later, Parliament voted to flood the land at the Welsh-speaking village of Capel Celyn, near Bala. This would create the Llyn Celyn reservoir and would supply water to Liverpool. Many people protested in anger but they lost. Villagers were forced to leave their homes. In 1965, over three square kilometres of land was flooded, including a school, post office, chapel and cemetery.

North Wales Today and Tomorrow...

The history of North Wales can be discovered and enjoyed in lots of ways. You can walk around the old Roman fort, explore the castles and visit the slate quarrying towns. Remember that the history of North Wales is about the people who lived through difficult or exciting or dangerous times – people such as Gwyr, Marius, Constance, Agnes and Grace.

Portmeirion, Llandudno and other tourist hotspots bring £1.8 billion to North Wales each year and provide over 37,000 jobs.

Edward I's impressive castles, such as the one at Caernarfon, are now popular tourist attractions.

The Eisteddfod is one of Wales's oldest festivals, and helps keep the Welsh culture and language alive and thriving. Do you think Eisteddfodau will still be going in 100 or 1,000 years' time?

Mount Snowdon is the tallest mountain in Wales and is described as the 'busiest mountain in Britain'.

SPOT THIS!

Tramcars have been taking visitors up Llandudno's Great Orme since 1902. But can you find the tram station?

This village on Anglesey has the longest place name in Europe. Can you say the whole name?

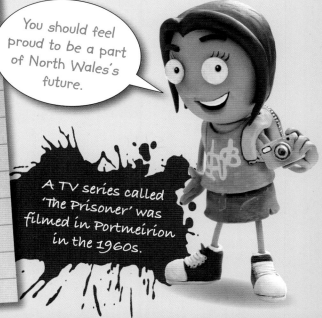

Slate mining has been a part of life for generations of families in North Wales. Hear the Story of Slate at the National Slate Museum in Llanberis.

How will they know?

Will North Wales always look like it does today? How will future generations know what it was like when we lived here? The Internet is a great way of recording what it's like where we live. Photos, blogs and stories from tourists who visit places like Snowdonia and Llandudno all spread the word about our wonderful North Wales. Or maybe you'll be famous one day and put your own part of North Wales on the map!

You should feel proud to be a part of North Wales's future.

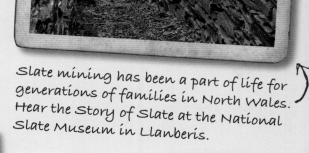

A TV series called 'The Prisoner' was filmed in Portmeirion in the 1960s.

Glossary

AD – a short way of writing the Latin words anno Domini, which mean 'in the year of our Lord', i.e. after the birth of Christ.

Aqueduct – a structure (often a bridge) that carries water over a long distance.

Archaeologist – a person who studies the past by examining buildings and objects left behind by previous people and cultures.

Auxiliary – someone or something that helps another.

BC – initials meaning 'Before Christ', used for the period of time before Christ was born.

Barbican – the outer defence of a castle.

Bard – a poet or storyteller who passes stories from one generation to the next.

Benedictine – a monk or nun who joins the Christian religious community that follows the teachings of St Benedict.

Blacksmith – a person who makes things with iron, such as horseshoes and swords.

Christian – anyone who believes Christ is the son of God and follows his teachings.

Cistercian – a member of a very strict order of monks founded in France.

Eisteddfod – a Welsh festival that celebrates music, poetry and performance.

Emblem – a badge or symbol that means something special. For example, a dove is an emblem of peace.

Evacuate – having to leave your home and live somewhere else for safety.

Excavation – a site where archaeologists dig up buried objects in order to find out more about the past.

Frieze – a decorated border or band along the top of a wall.

Hill fort – a fort or camp that's built on a hill to give better protection from the enemy.

Legion – a military unit in the Roman army of between 3,000 and 6,000 men.

Mason – a person who works with, and makes things from, stone. Mason is short for stonemason.

Monastery – a place where monks live and worship.

Monk – a male member of a religious community that has rules of poverty, chastity and obedience. There are many different orders of monks.

Normans – people from Normandy in France who invaded England and became powerful in the 11th century.

Quarryman – a man who works in a quarry, where people dig or blast stone out of the ground.

Rationing – during World War Two, certain foods were scarce. You were given a Ration Book showing how much of this food you could buy every week.

Rushes – the stalks of thick grasses laid on the stone floors of houses. Rushes could also be used to weave baskets.

Sacrifice – killing an animal or person as an offering to a god.

Swaddling – strips of cloth used to wrap around babies to keep them warm.

Ward – an area of ground inside the walls of a castle.

Wattle and daub – twigs and branches woven together and plastered with mud (and sometimes dung), then used as a building material.

Index

Acknowledgements

The author and publishers would like to thank the Codman family for their generous help in supplying pictures of their Punch and Judy show.

The publishers would like to thank the following people and organizations for their permission to reproduce material on the following pages:
Cover: by kind permission of Cadw, Welsh Assembly Government; p5: National Museum of Wales; p6: Clwyd-Powys Archaeological Trust, National Museum of Wales; p8: National Museum of Wales; p9: National Museum of Wales; p10: Fishbourne Museum in Portsmouth; p11: Fishbourne Museum in Portsmouth; p13: Robert Estall Photo Agency/Alamy; p15: Cadw, Welsh Assembly Government; p16: Cadw, Welsh Assembly Government; p18: Ale flashero/Wikipedia; p19: Cadw, Welsh Assembly Government; p21: Gwydir Castle; p22: Gordon Casbeard, National Slate Museum, Llanberis; p23: Codman's Punch and Judy of Llandudno, Bodelwyddan Castle; p24: Bodelwyddan Castle; p25: National Slate Museum, Llanberis; p26: Graham A. Stephen; p28: Gail Johnson/Shutterstock, Cadw, Welsh Assembly Government, Keith Morris/National Eisteddfod of Wales.

All other images copyright of Hometown World

Written by Catherine Robinson
Educational consultant: Neil Thompson
Local history consultant: Robin Evans
Designed by Stephen Prosser

Illustrated by Kate Davies, Dynamo Ltd, Peter Kent,
John MacGregor, Leighton Noyes and Tim Sutcliffe.
Additional photographs by Alex Long

First published by HOMETOWN WORLD in 2011
Hometown World Ltd
7 Northumberland Buildings
Bath BA1 2JB

www.hometownworld.co.uk

Copyright © Hometown World Ltd 2011

hb ISBN 978-1-84993-151-9
pb ISBN 978-1-84993-152-6

BRANCH	DATE
CN	5/11